TOMORROW NEVER KNOWS:

The
BEATLES'
LAST CONCERT

TERRA FIRMA

Library of Congress Card Number: 87-080730

ISBN Number: 0-943249-02-3

Printed in Japan

Typeset by The Writer's Center, Bethesda, MD

Published by Terra Firma Books
       2215-R Market St. #444
       San Francisco, CA 94114

10 9 8 7 6 5 4 3 2 1

FIRST EDITION

TOMORROW NEVER KNOWS:

The BEATLES' LAST CONCERT

BY

ERIC LEFCOWITZ

WITH PHOTOS BY

JIM MARSHALL

Design by Stephane Krieshok
Cover Design by Meletios Peppas

I would like to acknowledge the many people who have assisted me on this project, including Yolanda Adra, David Bacon, Corey Busch, Jody Carpenter, Carlos Deza, Ben Fong Torres, Susan Griffin, Barry Hood, Penelope Houston, KSFO/KYA-FM, Let It Be Records, Norman Maslov, Bob McClay, Sarah Robinson, Anita Sethi, Harold Silen, San Francisco Graphic Reproduction, Pamela Brunger Scott, Terence Tumbale, Cliff Yamasaki and Dave Zimmer. For the interviews included in this book, I would like to thank Joan Baez, Raechel Donahue, Philip Elwood, Mimi Fariña, Mort Feld, Vern Miller and Gene Nelson. For support above and beyond the call of duty, I would further like to acknowledge my gratitude and love for each and every Lefcowitz, Freedgood and Sethi that I know. Also further thanks to Duane Dimock, Matt Mates, John Javna, Peter Handel, Ron Turner, and the B-town boys.

TABLE OF CONTENTS

INTRODUCING: THE BEATLES

While researching a previous book, I had the good fortune to be introduced to photographer Jim Marshall. At first I did not recognize his name, but when I saw his work, I instantly recognized the images—Jimi Hendrix on his knees squirting lighter fluid on his flaming guitar at the Monterey Pop Festival; Janis Joplin caressing a bottle of Southern Comfort backstage at the Fillmore. Annie Leibovitz once wrote, "Jim Marshall is *the* rock'n'roll photographer." She was right.

As a long-time Beatles aficionado, I was even more thrilled to find out that Jim had also been the official photographer for the Beatles' last concert at Candlestick Park in 1966. Thumbing through the proof sheets of that historic night was like re-entering the event itself. Like short little bursts of Beatle history, every frame of every photo captured a split-second nuance or emotion.

After a little research, however, I discovered that the Beatles' August 29, 1966 performance in San Francisco was something of a non-event. Tired from their grueling and chaotic tour, the Beatles had run their thirty-minute, eleven-song set with surgeon-like precision. Certainly, the reaction from the 25,000 cold-braving fans in attendance was considerably tamer than previous years. Outdoors, in a cavernous baseball stadium, the magic and intimacy had been lost.

The real significance of the Candlestick Park show, of course, would not become apparent for a few more years. Only after the group's bitter demise several years later would it become clear that August 29, 1966 represented something bigger—it was the end of Beatlemania in its purest and most innocent form. Jim Marshall likes to call it "the last hard day's night." His photos tell the rest of the story.

Photographer Jim Marshall (standing) poses backstage with Ringo Starr at Candlestick Park.

The Beatles' Candlestick Park poster was designed by artist Wes Wilson, whose wild, psychedelic designs became a hallmark of the San Francisco music scene in the late Sixties.

1966: IT'S ALL TOO MUCH

A watershed year in politics, lifestyles and culture, the year 1966 in many ways mirrored the happenstance and fortunes of the four Beatles.

It was a year in which innocence was lost—Masters and Johnson released "Human Sexual Response", shattering sexual myths of the past. A *Time* magazine cover asked, "Is God Dead?". Public protest over the escalating war in Vietnam spilled over onto the streets and the campuses, while ghettos seethed in white-hot anger over the injustices of racism.

On the brighter side, popular culture scaled increasingly-bold peaks of capitalistic self-expression. The Scott Paper company began selling disposable paper dresses for one dollar. New TV shows such as "Star Trek" boldly went where no television executive had gone before. And strange new garage/acid bands with names such as the Thirteenth Floor Elevators, the Seeds and the Count Five, all had surprise Top Forty hits. Yes, something was afoot—a chemical change was in the air (and the punch as well).

In San Francisco, the new year was ushered in on January 21-23 in a prescient gathering of the tribes dubbed "The Trips Festival." Produced by then-fledgling promoter Bill Graham, the Trips Festival was actually the collective brain product of Ken Kesey's Merry Pranksters, Stewart "Whole Earth" Brand, Allen Ginsberg and a group named the Warlocks (a.k.a. the Grateful Dead). The three day festival of music, light shows and "anything goes" anarchy launched a new era of pyschedelia. One week later, the U.S. government began federal regulation of LSD.

Beneath the giddy, day-glo rush of activity was a central catalyzing event—the Vietnam War. The conflict in Southeast Asia had polarized a once-somnolent nation into divisive and bitter battle. Two camps quickly emerged; it was hawk versus dove, old versus young, square versus hip.

As usual, the Beatles were right in the pipeline—riding the crest of current events, social change and fashion. The former mop tops would also lose a lot of their innocence in 1966. As the year began, the group's latest album, *Rubber Soul*, rose to the top of the charts. The cover art, alone, reflected a breakthrough in the group's self-image. Exaggerated, bubble-like graphics and a slightly out-of-focus fisheye photo of the group portended new creative heights for the band.

Haight Street in San Francisco, where all you needed was love. The imminent rise of flower power coincided perfectly with the Beatles' initial forays into psychedelia.

And they delivered the goods. Although *Rubber Soul* is often singled out for the introduction of the sitar (via "Norwegian Wood"), it was really more significant for establishing new ground rules for what an album could be—a unified and cohesive vision from first track to last. Brian Wilson would soon meet that challenge with his magnum opus, *Pet Sounds*. At the same time, the Beatles had taken one giant step away from the roots rock'n'roll that had forged their initial mania. *Rubber Soul* was an album to be listened—not danced—to; both critics and society hailed it as a work of art.

Things had changed drastically—the former scruffy Liverpudlians of a few years back were now designated Members of the British Empire, flirting dangerously with across-the-board acceptance. The memory of Elvis' defection to show business was still fresh in the minds of the four Beatles—they did not want to follow the King to the throne of the golden-oldies circuit.

"We can't go on holding hands forever," John Lennon admitted to journalist Maureen Cleave of the London *Evening Standard* in an interview published on March 4, 1966. "We have been Beatles as best we ever will be—those four jolly lads. But we're not those people any more. We are old men...we've got to find something else to do. Paul says it's like leaving school and finding a job. It's just like school, actually, because you have the group to lean on, and then suddenly you find you're on your own."

THE DREADED DOWNFALL

Cleave's interview, which would later erupt into the great "we're bigger than Jesus" controversy, revealed a world-weary Lennon, ready to abdicate his crown: "We sort of half hope for The Downfall—a nice downfall. Then we would just be a pleasant old memory."

The venomous British press had been waiting anxiously for the first signs of this much-anticipated "downfall." When the group's "Paperback Writer"/"Rain" single was released in June, 1966, the papers duly noted that it was the Beatles' first British single since "She Loves You" to not hit number one its first week in release. Near perfection, it seems, was not quite enough.

Furthermore, the group's main rivals, the Rolling Stones, had recently begun to win headlines formerly reserved for Beatlemania. The Stones' brusque "we piss anywhere" attitude had captured the imaginations of rebellious youths everywhere. In terms of counterculture cool and titillation on the Top Forty, the Stones' "Paint It Black" had clearly aced out the Beatles' "Paperback Writer" in the spring of 1966. The Stones' manager, Andrew Loog Oldham, realized the golden rule of hype: any press, even bad press, was good press. This was hardly the approach of the Beatles' genteel manager Brian Epstein. Controversy, in Epstein's view, was to be avoided at all cost—he wanted the Beatles to project a wholesome, fun-loving spirit, a la "A Hard Day's Night."

How ironic, then, that the Beatles' upcoming summer tour would be mired knee-deep in muck—some of it unintentional, but much of it the design of John Lennon. Clearly, the outspoken Beatle had no interest in sitting back and watching Jagger and company win the "can you top this?" battle of outrageous behavior.

Lennon's opening salvo was the "butcher sleeve." Incensed that their creative license had once again been violated by Capitol Records on the fast-buck *Yesterday and Today* album (which was nothing more than a cheap pastiche of leftover tracks from *Help!*, *Rubber Soul* and the soon-to-be-released *Revolver*), the Beatles designed an album cover whose message could not be ignored—that is, posing with severed baby parts and bloody lumps of meat. Lennon told *Melody Maker* magazine that the cover (which at the last second was pasted over—it's amazing that it ever got *that* far) was "as valid as Vietnam."

The "butcher sleeve" would soon seem like a minor snafu in comparison to what awaited the Beatles, however. In his frank interview with Maureen Cleave, Lennon had broached the touchy subject of organized religion. His comments: "Christianity will go. It will vanish and shrink. I needn't argue about that. I'm right and I will be proved right. We're more popular than Jesus now...Jesus was all right but his disciples were thick and ordinary. It's them twisting it that ruins it for me."

Twist and shout.

Baby, you're a rich man, too: Brian Epstein (left), the Beatles' manager, was greatly affected by the group's decision to stop touring. Almost one year to the day of the Candlestick Park show, Epstein died of an overdose of sleeping pills. (Right) The infamous Datebook cover. Surprised by the ruckus they had created, the magazine milked the controversy for all it was worth—including a follow-up issue defending their actions.

YOU KNOW IT AIN'T EASY

John Lennon's off-handed comments to Maureen Cleave had been all but ignored by the British public when published in the London *Evening Standard* on March 4, 1966. The English, with their long history of shock effect—from the Goon Show and later Monty Python and the Sex Pistols—had hardened sensibilities when it came to such sacrilege; they barely batted an eye.

In the United States, however, acts of blasphemy are usually met with swift and severe punishment. Therefore, when an American teen-zine named *Datebook* decided to print Lennon's "Jesus" remarks out-of-context on their front cover, a mighty hail of fire-and-brimstone was all but inevitable.

The actual outbreak of the hysteria was in Birmingham, Alabama, where a radio station disc jockey named Tommy James began to read Lennon's inflammatory remarks over the airwaves of WAQY. It may have been a cheap publicity stunt, but it was also an effective one—James' announcement that he would hire "a tree-grinding machine to pulverize Beatles records to dust" drew national press attention.

The floodgates had been opened. Almost instantaneously, similarly low-rated radio stations jumped on the boycott bandwagon, removing all Beatles records from their playlist. At the same time, Beatle bonfires were quickly organized by outraged citizens and opportunistic holy roller types. Not everyone was against the Beatles, however. One station, KLUE, in Shreveport, Louisiana was knocked off the air by a bolt of lightning one day after organizing a Beatle bonfire. Another radio station, WSAC, in Ft. Worth, Kentucky, actually played Beatles' music for the *first* time, to show, in their words, "our contempt for hypocrisy personified."

Contrary to a commonly-held belief, the bannings and burnings were not concentrated solely in the South—even "intellectual" New York and "laid-back" California had their minor outbreaks. Nor was the furor only in America—the group was banned altogether by Spain and South Africa (although the latter case may have been in retribution for the Beatles' refusal to play Sun City due to that country's policy of apartheid).

To make matters worse, the Beatles' upcoming North American tour, which was only a matter of weeks away, was in serious jeopardy of being cancelled. To the four members, still recuperating in London from the opening leg of their European/ Far East tour, the latest controversy was a bad omen, indeed. Already, their recent dates had been a major fiasco. The tour had begun in late June, with three stops in West Germany. Crowd violence and riots, both inside and outside the concerts, had marred the Beatles' return to the Old Country. Even their old stomping grounds, Hamburg, was not immune to the mayhem.

Next stop had been Japan—but before the group could make it to the Land of Rising Sun, their flight was forced to land in Anchorage, Alaska due to a typhoon. Once in Japan, the Beatles found themselves confined to their hotel rooms, protected by a massive security force, which according to *Life* magazine, totalled 8,500 police and firemen. The extraordinary show of force had been necessitated by Japan's right-wing Patriotic Party, who were protesting the Beatles' performances at the sacred Budo Kan Hall.

Japan was merely a prelude, however, to what would follow in the Philippines. After playing two outdoor shows in Manila, the group indiscriminately snubbed a party being thrown by Philippine First Lady, Imelda Marcos. The next day, as the Beatles attempted to leave the country, a blood-thirsty mob met them at the airport. For a few hair-raising seconds, the Beatles were jostled about by angry bystanders, before fleeing for their safety in an awaiting jet. To add insult to injury, the group left the Philippines without getting paid.

The unseemly turn of events had severely shaken the Beatles' confidence in their manager Brian Epstein. Even before the tour had made it to America, the four Beatles were already giving serious thought to ending live appearances altogether—a move that would virtually eliminate the last vestiges of Epstein's control within the group. Simply put, touring had become intolerable.

On April 13, 1966, San Fran- isco Chronicle *columnist, Charles McCabe, became the first American journalist to comment on Lennon's theo- logical remarks in his article, "Do Beatles Top Christ?" (right).*

Our Fearless Correspondent

Do Beatles Top Christ?

Charles McCabe

"CHRISTIANITY will go. It will vanish and shrink. I needn't argue about that; I'm right and I will be proved right. We're more popular than Jesus now."

Talking was Mr. John Lennon, the Beatle. He was talking to Maureen Cleave, an interviewer for the Evening Standard, of London. He did not say he was speaking corporately, so we may assume his sentiments are strictly his own. He added:

"Jesus was all right but his disciples were thick and ordinary."

There is no doubt at all the lad was talking seriously. What are we to make of it all? Can the acclaim of millions of goslings so affect a lad that he can patronize the greatest man produced by Western civilization; and suggest in all gravity that what he and his mates do is more popular—and ergo, more important than what Jesus Christ did?

★ ★ ★

I DON'T THINK the young fellow is mad, or anything. He is a victim of belief, which often erodes intelligence. It is a belief often common to those who reap the strange rewards the theatrical life can yield. He think's he's God. Naturally, he's a bit jealous of those notices his Son has been getting all through these centuries.

Since he's a nice kid, I hope he gets over his delusion before it begins to hurt him. But there it is: the lightweights who don't want to play Hamlet want to play God.

I take it as given doctrine that all actors are emotional cripples. The greatest actors are very crippled indeed.

Why would a man pound out onto a stage and make a fool of himself—and from Olivier to Lennie Bruce that's what they all are doing—had he not somewhere along the line been deprived of normal quotient of love? It is a black childhood that leads a man to the bright lights.

★ ★ ★

THE ACTOR stands up there, and with his bag of tricks, extorts love outrageously from his audience. The theatrical expressions "to milk a line" or a joke or an audience, are not accidental. For handclaps and foot stomps read "love I never had."

When the actor gets enough of this fake love he can keep his life in equipoise, get his work done and be a useful member of the community. Sometimes, even, he can wed another person properly.

Mostly the people in the theater who achieve this emotional equipoise are the distinguished supporting players, who are nearly all delightful people.

But even an actor can get more fake love than he can support. In this he is inferior to the politician—a tougher breed of cat, who can withstand any amount of love, and still smile, smile, smile.

★ ★ ★

I SUGGEST THIS is what happened to young Mr. Lennon. He has been so loved that he has been besotted by love. A bright Liverpudlian youth had donned the homespun chiton of a Greek sage. A kid still damp behind the ears dismisses out of hand the only man whose message has been taken seriously by Western humanity in the last 20 centuries.

Mr. Lennon has every right not to believe in Christianity. After all, the mad Mr. Nietzsche said the last Christian died on the cross. And the excessively sane Mr. Bernard Shaw said that Christianity had not failed, because it had never been tried. Even your fearless correspondent is not sure he has met enough Christians in his time to form a pick-up stick ball team.

But the young Beatle had better pipe down. Unless he purges himself of the sin of pride he may find he is entirely left out when the Top Forty are picked out at the pearly gates. And we can guess Who will be doing the picking.

YOU KNOW HOW HARD IT CAN BE

After returning from Manila for a month's vacation, Harrison dryly told reporters, "we're going to have a couple of weeks to recuperate before we go and get beaten up by the Americans." Whether in jest or not, Harrison's statement would soon be realized—a few weeks later, the Beatles' summer tour would be steeped in conflict thanks to John Lennon's regrettable allusions to Jesus Christ.

No one was taking the news worse than Brian Epstein. Still ailing from the "thrilla in Manila", Epstein rose from his sick-bed to fly to New York on August 6 in hopes of "quelling the storm" over Lennon's remarks. Ironically, the mushrooming controversy provided the petulant manager with a perfect opportunity to prove his managerial mettle. In a hastily-arranged press conference, Epstein announced: "If any promoter wants to cancel, I would not stand in his way." Furthermore, he declared his willingness to part with $1,000,000 to cancel the tour completely.

Epstein's gambit hit paydirt. No promoter would dare invoke the wrath of 30,000 ticket-holding teenagers (although, later on, many probably wish they had). The only problem spot was the Beatles' one date in the Bible Belt—Memphis, Tennessee; home of the Sun Record sound so lovingly duplicated in the Beatles' tributes to Carl Perkins. William Ingram, the mayor of Memphis, announced his intentions to block the Beatles' upcoming pair of shows, citing his "duty to protect Memphians against the Beatles' use of the public coliseum to ridicule anyone's religion." In all likelihood, the reaction in Memphis had as much to do with the Beatles' cancellation of a recording date in the city earlier that year as it did with Lennon's comments in *Datebook*. Either way, despite the political grandstanding, the show—and the tour—would go on as planned.

"What was the reaction in 'Frisco?" McCabe asked incredulously in a follow-up article concerning the nationwide Lennon controversy. "And its youth? And its clergy? And its swingin' disc jockeys, those shamans of the affluent society? Nothingsville, that's what."

All in all, the damage, thus far, had been negligible (although shares in Northern Songs, Ltd. stock did take a brief slide). Advance ticket sales—which had hardly been bigger than Jesus to begin with—actually took a slight upturn in the wake of the theological brouhaha. Moreover, several religious figures had actually stepped forward to *defend* Lennon's remarks. The London *Catholic Herald*, for example, commented that Lennon had given Christians "a well-placed kick where it was most needed." Even *L'Osservatore*, the Vatican newspaper, agreed—stating with authority that "the matter is closed." But was it?

The answer, as the Beatles would soon find out, was no. For despite the many apologies and explanations, one got the feeling that all was forgiven but not forgotten. Twenty years later the memory of the debacle was still fresh in Paul McCartney's mind, when he told *Musician* magazine: "He (Lennon) meant that the church congregations were in decline. But you take it out of context, you send it to Selma, Alabama, you put it on the front page and you've got little eleven-year-olds thumping on your coach saying, 'Blasphemer! Devil worshiper!' I'll never forget the sight of a little blonde kid trying to get to us, and he would have done it, if he'd have got to us. I mean, at eleven, what does this kid know about life and religion? He'd just been whipped up."

Perhaps the best summation of the whole affair was offered by British media figure, David Frost, who wrote in the London *Spectator*. "Should not on principle, a civilized society be beyond the point where one paragraph by anyone about anything can produce this sort of hysteria?"

In 1966, the Beatles conspicuously avoided the crazy airport scenes from previous years. In San Francisco, they taxied one mile from the main terminal. Only a few lucky fans (left) watched as the group posed one last time for the obligatory photo opportunity on the airplane steps (right).

ARRIVE ALIVE

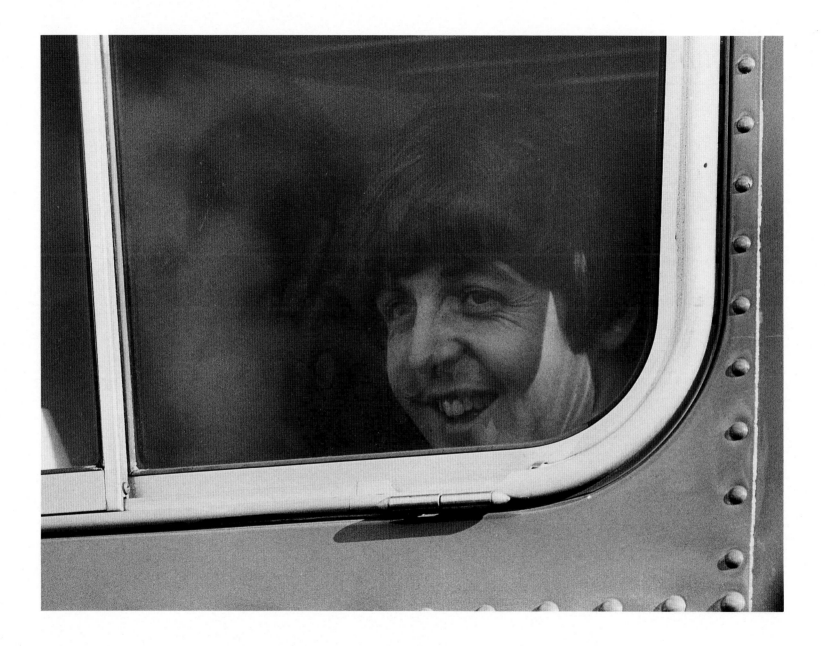

CANDLESTICK PARK: FACTS AND FIGURES

Candlestick Park is located in the southeast corner of San Francisco at Candlestick Point. Infamous for its wind conditions, the 'Stick is directly adjacent the shoreline of the San Francisco Bay. The following are some of Candlestick Park's more memorable events:

1959: Groundbreaking ceremonies. Name is chosen from 15,000 ballots submitted in a name-the-stadium contest.

1960: On April 12, the San Francisco Giants baseball team plays its first game at Candlestick Park. Capacity: 42,500.

1962: A gust of wind knocks pitcher Stu Miller off the mound during a nationally-televised All-Star game.
The New York Yankees beat the San Francisco Giants in the seventh game of the World Series.

1966: On August 29, the Beatles play their final concert.

1972: The outfield area is enclosed in an effort to lessen gusting winds and up the stadium's seating capacity to 58,000.

1982: Candlestick Park hosts its first concert since the Beatles. The group: the Rolling Stones.

1984: Baseball fans are given a badge of courage, called "Croix de Candlestick," for staying during extra-inning night games.

1986: On August 29, the San Francisco Giants hold a "Beatle Night" to celebrate the 20th anniversary of the Beatles' last show.

1987: Twenty years after John Lennon plays Candlestick, Pope John Paul II holds a mass at Candlestick Park.

On August 29, 1986, the San Francisco Giants baseball team held a "Beatles Night" to celebrate the twentieth anniversary of the Beatles' last show at Candlestick Park. A commemorative plaque (above) currently resides in the Stadium Club.

THE WAY THINGS ARE GOING

Ready or not, the Beatles' third American tour was scheduled to begin on August 12. Just one week before, the group's seventh album, *Revolver*, had been released. Its original title, *Abracadabra*, had described it to a tee: it was a magic show of seemingly perfect musicianship. Even the ever-churlish British press had to agree with McCartney's boast to *Melody Maker*—"They'll never copy this!"

The problem was that the Beatles, themselves, would have a hard time duplicating the songs off *Revolver* in concert—particularly since they had not rehearsed any of them. Even the current hit single, "Eleanor Rigby"/"Yellow Submarine" could not be performed, much to the group's chagrin.

By 1966, the Beatles' performances had reached a stultifying regularity. Shielded by the incessant jet-like screams of Beatlemania, the group could practically sleep-walk through a show—and often did. Beyond just showing up, all that counted were the gate receipts and percentages. As Hunter Davies later wrote: "They hated what they were doing. They disliked dragging around the world, appearing publicly in a glass box like a peep show. They thought it was a farce, a mockery."

And yet, publicly, the four Beatles did not let their frustrations show. Before leaving on their Far East tour, both Lennon and Starr were asked for their views on touring and growing older by *Melody Maker*. "I don't think I'm too old to be a Beatle," Lennon replied. "I never think about being a Beatle until I'm on tour or something. The rest of the time I'm just me." Ringo admitted that "I sometimes do think I'm a bit old to be going onstage doing this. Then I look around at all the other people doing the same and I don't feel so bad."

As for any plans to stop touring, Lennon was doubtful: "Not the way the fans keep moaning about not seeing us all the time." Ringo simply replied, "No."

Despite the public displays, the prospects for the group's upcoming fourteen-day, seventeen-show tour could best be described as grim. Two weeks in the sweltering American summer playing cavernous ballparks full of screaming fans sounded like a death sentence. After the near-disaster in the Philippines, the Beatles now genuinely feared for their lives. Already, a medium had prophesized that the group would die in a plane crash—sacks full of hate mail only fueled their paranoia.

On August 12, the group reluctantly boarded their Pan Am flight from Heathrow Airport to Boston. Seeing them off was a group of concerned fans who had circulated a petition begging the group to cancel the tour. "John, please don't go," *Newsweek* reported one fan screaming, "They'll kill you."

As soon as the group arrived in Chicago, the four Beatles were hustled into an overflowing press conference to offer their rote apologies. According to a UPI reporter, the group "appeared pale and tired" as Lennon attempted to explain his remarks. "I suppose if I said television was more popular than Jesus, I would have gotten away with it," he explained feebly. "I am sorry I opened my mouth."

It was an inauspicious start, to be sure, for a Beatles' concert tour. The witty repartee and good-natured hijinx of past news conferences were now gone, lost in the bright glare of the television cameras. Lennon's momentary indiscretion had cost the group its first truly negative publicity. The ramifications were clear: now that the group was no longer lovable mop tops, a good part of the American public—particularly parents—were ready, willing and waiting to skewer the Beatles.

THE BEATLES' 1966 NORTH AMERICAN TOUR SCHEDULE

August 12: Two shows at the International Amphitheatre, Chicago, Illinois.

August 13: Two shows at Olympia Stadium, Detroit, Michigan.

August 14: One show at Municipal Stadium, Cleveland, Ohio.

August 15: One show at DC Stadium, Washington, DC.

August 16: One show at JFK Stadium, Philadelphia, Pennsylvania.

August 17: Two shows at Maple Leaf Gardens, Toronto, Canada.

August 18: One show at Suffolk Downs Racetrack, Boston, Massachusetts.

August 19: Two shows at the Mid-South Coliseum, Memphis, Tennessee.

August 21: One show at Crosly Field, Cincinnati, Ohio.
One show at Busch Stadium, St. Louis, Missouri.

August 23: One show at Shea Stadium, New York, New York.

August 25: Two shows at the Seattle Coliseum, Seattle, Washington.

August 28: One show at Dodger Stadium, Los Angeles, California.

August 29: One show at Candlestick Park, San Francisco, California.

ROLL UP: THE MISERY TOUR

Despite the tidal wave of bad press, the August 12 opening shows in Chicago—with a total of 25,000 fans in attendance—went off without a hitch. The next day in Detroit was a similar success. In Cleveland, however, the old fears of being mobbed were once again renewed. In the middle of "Day Tripper," thousands of fans broke through security lines and rushed the stage, forcing the Beatles to literally flee for their lives. The concert was delayed for thirty-three minutes while authorities attempted to restore order. At the end of the Cleveland show, another mob attacked the Beatles' limousines. Kenny Everett reported the hysteria in *Melody Maker*: "Hundreds of them broke out again and dashed for the car. Four policemen and detectives threw themselves on the car—it looked just like the Kennedy assassination all over again."

Fortunately for the group, the next few shows—in Washington, D.C., Philadelphia, Toronto and Boston—were trouble-free; although a few Ku Klux Klan had shown up at the group's concert in the nation's capital. On August 19, the group made their much-anticipated visit to Memphis, Tennessee. Picketing outside their concert was a Christian Youth Rally, eight thousand strong, including those perennial cross-burners, the KKK. Nobody was singing "Love Me Do."

A palpable tension could be felt at the Beatles' two performances at Memphis' Mid South Coliseum. The Beatles' handlers, particularly Brian Epstein, were horrified by the specter of violence. In one heart-stopping moment, their nightmare seemed to have materialized as a cherry bomb exploded onstage at one of the Memphis shows. For a split-second it sounded as if a sniper had taken a shot at the group. Lennon, the most likely target for such an attack, nonchalantly checked for any flesh wounds and continued playing.

The tour hit its nadir the following day in Cincinnati, where heavy rainfall threatened to cancel the outdoor show at Crosley Field. When Mal Evans, the Beatles' loyal roadie, was thrown twenty feet across the stage while plugging in the amps, it was wisely decided that the threat of electrocution was too great and the show was cancelled.

Clearly, Brian Epstein's ballpark strategy was turning into a quagmire of immense proportions. Not only were the logistics difficult—weather, sound, and security were all unpredictable entities—but local promoters (who were forced to hand over 65%

Revolver was further proof that the Beatles had grown leaps and bounds from their initial mania. Still, some pre-teen fans only saw the cartoon caricatures of old. "We're not those people any more," Lennon claimed. "We are old men."

of the gate receipts to the Beatles) were literally taking a bath. In Philadelphia, for example, only 21,000 seats out of 60,000 had been sold. Noting the less-than-full houses, *Billboard* magazine ran the headline "Beatlemania Turns To Beatle-waneia", stating (incorrectly), "it seems that the Beatles have begun the long, slow downward journey."

Things were not getting any easier, either. On August 21, the Beatles were forced to play a noon-time make-up gig in Cincinnati and then fly off to St. Louis for another show that night. Reportedly, the strain of the events had taken a toll on Paul McCartney, who was physically ill after the Cincinnati show. In St. Louis, another downfall of rain made electrocution a distinct possibility. "Let the support acts go on," Lennon cracked backstage, "and if they don't get frazzled, I don't mind having a go."

After St. Louis, the group flew to New York for a day of rest and relaxation—they were bruised and beaten, but at least they were alive. Vacation was brief, however, as two teenage girls threatened to jump from the ledge of the twenty-second floor of the Beatles' hotel if they were not allowed to meet the group. They were eventually

coaxed from the ledge and taken to a hospital for observation.

In many ways, the Beatles' 1966 visit to the Big Apple epitomized the entire tour. New York, of course, had been host to many Beatle epiphanies—Ed Sullivan, Kennedy Airport, Carnegie Hall, Shea Stadium. This time, however, only nine fans were there to greet them at LaGuardia Airport; only 500 kids showed up at their hotel, compared to 10,000 from the year before; and, most significantly, sales were down by 11,000 for their repeat performance at Shea Stadium.

Tony Barrow, the Beatles' press agent, later wrote in "The Beatles Book" fan magazine: "One year ago I found the group's first Shea date the most exciting of any Beatle concert I had ever seen anywhere in the world. There wasn't quite the same magic this time around. That's the strange part about the 1966 tour. Quite clearly it's the biggest money-spinner in the history of pop music, but box-office records aside, all the hassles before and during this trip seem to have robbed the atmosphere of a little magic."

Even the publicity-minded Epstein could be heard admitting the group was "not the novelty they were." Still, one bit of good news was there to greet the Beatles in New York—a newly-minted gold record for *Revolver*. There was no time to celebrate, however, as the group caught a commercial red-eye flight from New York to Los Angeles, where a fully-furnished mansion awaited them.

Nestled away in the seclusion of Beverly Hills, the Beatles enjoyed a much-needed respite from the rigors of touring. The group threw several pool-side parties at their rented mansion, inviting the local cognoscenti of California pop—the Byrds, the Beach Boys, and the Mamas and the Papas. Derek Taylor, their ex-publicity whiz, and Joan Baez also joined the festivities.

Not surprisingly, the group was reluctant to leave the luxurious spread for a pair of shows in Seattle on August 25. A bumpy three-hour flight did not help matters since the group was, by now, highly superstitious of flying. In Seattle, the band cranked out two more perfunctory performances. "I reckon we could send out four waxwork dummies of ourselves and that would satisfy the crowds," Lennon had said earlier in the year. "Beatles concerts are nothing to do with music any more. They're just bloody tribal rites."

If Lennon was open and candid about the sorry state of affairs, manager Brian Epstein was quite the opposite—he refused to publicly admit that the less-riotous crowds and empty seats meant that the Beatles popularity had waned. "This tour compares phenomenally well with last year's," Epstein said in a press statement before the group's August 28 performance at L.A.'s Dodger Stadium. "Here in Los Angeles, for example, 36,000 people saw the Beatles at the Hollywood Bowl. Today's concert at Dodger Stadium is attracting ten thousand more."

What Epstein had failed to gauge, however, was the emotional swing from Hollywood Bowl to Dodger Stadium. Sure, the profits were up (the Beatles' reportedly netted a record 1.4 million dollars for the tour), but an essential quality had died: spontaneity. At the '64 and '65 Hollywood Bowl shows, there was a genuine outpouring—both give and take—of love and adulation. At Dodger Stadium in 1966, there was only mayhem. The group raced through the set, the fans came and went, the receipts were totalled. The song "Money" summed up the difference.

Fortunately, for everybody involved, only one show remained.

AND I WENT INTO A DREAM . . .

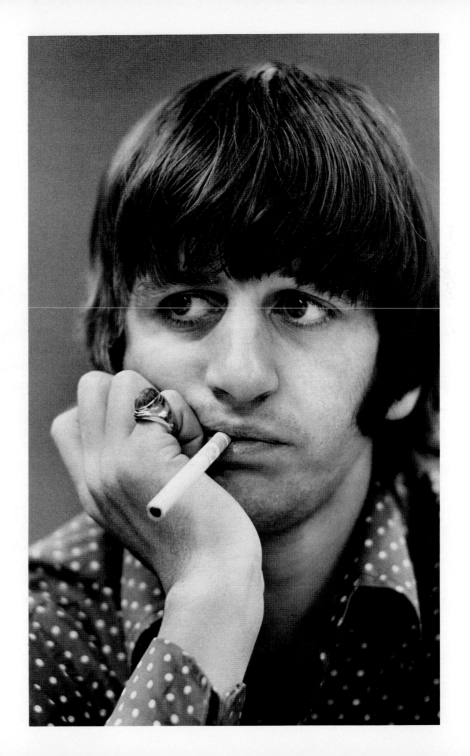

SAN FRANCISCO: OPEN YOUR GOLDEN GATE

Sometime in the mid-afternoon on August 29, the Beatles boarded their chartered American Airlines flight for the one-hour coastline hop from Los Angeles to San Francisco. Waiting at the San Francisco Airport terminal were scattered bands of Beatle diehards, hoping to catch an Instamatic glimpse of their heroes.

At approximately 5:25 PM, the group's jet landed at the airport and immediately taxied out of sight to the northeast end of the airfield to an old Pan Am terminal. There, they were greeted by a wall of grim-faced cops and fifty or so members of the local press. Reluctantly, the group assembled for the now-cliché photo opportunity of the Beatles waving and smiling from the plane steps—only this time there were no screaming crowds or banners, just an eerie calm.

It was a far different scene than 1964, when 9000 crazed teenagers had shown up at San Francisco Airport as the Beatles arrived in the United States for the opening shows on their first full-length American tour. At that time, San Francisco, like every city across the country, was caught up in a dementia known as Beatlemania. Even local civic officials had gone a little haywire, suggesting plans for a full-scale ticker tape parade (á là San Francisco's emotional tribute to General Douglas MacArthur, one decade before).

Ultimately, the plans were nixed, but George Harrison, in his autobiography, "I Me Mine," never forgot the hysteria. "Those tours in the United States were crazy," Harrison wrote. "The first big American trip, when we arrived in San Francisco, in 1964, they wanted to do a ticker tape parade and I remember saying, 'No, no, no.' That imagery of being shot. Kennedy, Beatlemania, madness. Talk about pressures."

Indeed, the Beatles' first airport arrival in San Francisco had very nearly careened out of control, as Mark Lewisohn describes in his book, "The Beatles Live!": "Still on the tarmac the group was herded into a limousine and driven 50 yards into a protective fenced enclosure which would allow the press photographers their required pictures. Suddenly the 9000 clamouring fans pressed all around the fencing started to push in unison, many fainting in the terrible crush. The Beatles, horrified,

managed to escape split seconds before the assemblage collapsed under the feet of shrieking fans."

On August 19, 1964, the Beatles performed their first San Francisco shows at the Cow Palace. The fever pitch of the group's visit was so intense that it spilled over into streets and their hotel. In fact, when one misfortunate woman was robbed in her hotel room, her cries for help were mistaken for the shrieks of a Beatle fan.

The hysteria surrounding the Beatles' first San Francisco appearance could not help but make an indelible impression upon the Beatles and their entourage. Writing in his autobiography, "Fifty Years Adrift," Derek Taylor, the group's press officer on the 1964 tour, recalls the Beatles' arrival in San Francisco fondly: "Seeing the Golden Gate for the first time and sky-scrapers and fast cars with fins driven by cigar-chomping big shots and little deuce coupes with California girls at the wheel, we began to feel enormously privileged. The air was heavy with late-summer warmth and Beatlemania, and we were ready for the greatest show on earth to begin."

(Right) Lennon at the Beatles' 1965 return engagement at the Cow Palace. In 1966, security was considerably tighter. Some of the 200 security guards (left) at Candlestick Park were ex-Oakland Raider football players.

THERE'S A RIOT GOING ON

The Beatles' next visit to San Francisco was no less hysterical *and* historical than their first. On August 31, 1965, the group played two tour-closing shows at the Cow Palace. In attendance, high above the rafters, was Ken (*One Flew Over The Cuckoo's Nest*) Kesey and his band of Merry Pranksters, stoned to the heavens on Owsley's infamous di-lysergic acid. Alongside Kesey was journalist Tom Wolfe, who later recorded the events in his book "The Electric Kool-Aid Acid Test."

Wolfe's giddy, wired-up account of Kesey's LSD-inspired visions is perhaps the most insightful—and harrowing—portrait of a Beatles performance ever captured in print. As the Beatles took the stage at the Cow Palace, Wolfe writes: "The whole front section of the arena becomes a writhing, seething mass of little girls waving their arms in the air, this mass of pink arms...it is like a single colonial animal with a thousand waving pink tentacles...vibrating a poison madness and filling the universe with the teen agony torn out of them."

In all actuality, Kesey was not hallucinating—the Beatles' evening show (the matinee had been staid by comparison) was a no-holds-barred battle royale. An inadequate and understaffed security force simply could not contain the overzealous fan reaction. The San Francisco *Chronicle* reported that "most of the teenage girls who broke through the police lines and reached the stage appeared overcome with the nearness to the Beatles and simply swooned onto the floor."

For the ones that did not swoon, the Beatles were fair game. One dexterous boy managed to leap onstage, grab Lennon's cap and dive back into the crowd before anyone had even noticed. The band, tired from the rigors of another full-length tour, were not amused by the hell-bent antics—twice they stopped the show in an effort to restore order. Already, touring had become a grind—and this was only 1965.

Amazingly, Kesey, in his LSD-haze, had come to the same conclusion about the Beatles' performance dilemma. He told Wolfe: "Control—it is perfectly obvious—they have brought this whole mass of human beings to the point where they are one, out of their skulls, one psyche, and they have utter control over them. But they don't know what in the hell to do with it, they haven't the first idea, and they will lose it."

Lose it they would, but a psychic connection between Kesey and the Beatles had been established; a year and a half later, it would resurface in the "Magical

The mad but Merry Prankster himself, Ken Kesey (right), would later influence the Beatles on their "Magical Mystery Tour" film. Literally high above the rafters of the Cow Palace in 1965, Kesey witnessed the "vibrating poison madness" of a Beatles concert.

Mystery Tour", the Beatles' much-maligned TV special, which featured psychedelic "Magic Bus" antics similar to those of Kesey's mad but Merry Pranksters.

DEPRESSING PRESS

Kesey's "Acid Tests" were one of many isolated "happenings" making a stir in the San Francisco underground in the mid-Sixties. By the time the Beatles returned in 1966, the city of San Francisco had already experienced the first tremors of the coming youth culture revolution. New clubs, such as the Avalon and Fillmore, had opened up to celebrate the dawning of a new, higher consciousness. The rock concert of old had been transformed into a brain-shattering mix of psychedelic light displays and day-glo fashions.

New bands—the Jefferson Airplane, Big Brother and the Holding Company, Great Society—had emerged from the vortex of the Haight-Ashbury district, singing strange, often atonal, songs to LSD-addled crowds. Droning guitars and looping bass signatures were now de rigueur, as were rambling, spaced- out instrumentals. The buzz was on.

Musically, the Beatles had arrived at the same signpost to the future; in fact, technically, they had arrived first. Lennon and Harrison's psychedelic dabblings on *Revolver* predate any San Francisco vinyl of significance (The Jefferson Airplane's *Takes Off* came out a few weeks later).

Ironically, the Beatles not only inherited the credit for tuning in, but shared in the blame for those who had turned on and dropped out (this, mind you, before *Sgt. Pepper*). One week before the Candlestick Park show in 1966, the San Francisco *Chronicle* ran a sensationalistic exposé called "Inside A Berkeley Drug Party", in which journalist/provocateur Nicholas Von Hoffman wrote: "The hard day's night was beginning . . . the pusher shot again and the needle upset the mid-Western girl. She walked out of the kitchen through the living room, where there was no furniture, only a blanket on the floor and the LSD canvases painted by a friend and a cheap record player spinning out the Beatles."

Then again, almost all advance press on the Beatles' 1966 tour had been negative. When the hype surrounding Lennon's "Jesus" comments began to lose the public's interest, reporters began baiting the group into talking about the Vietnam War (Brian Epstein had begged in vain that they avoid the issue). Eventually, as the group grew more dispirited by the utter banality—and occasional hostility—of the press gatherings, all official press conferences were cancelled. Of course, this move merely caused more bad press, particularly in San Francisco, where a young girl stricken with multiple sclerosis (whose operation had been paid for by a Beatles' benefit concert from the year before) missed out on her promised chance to present the Beatles with an honorary plaque.

Never ones to be demure, the San Francisco dailies were rife with Beatle-bashing articles in the week leading up to their 1966 appearance at Candlestick Park. One article in the San Francisco *Chronicle*, entitled "Beatles Coming—What A Difference" attempted to probe teenagers' changing feelings towards the group: "The schoolgirls have a problem...how can they relate to grown men who are beginning to look, in this era of hipster fashions and Robin Hood boots, as square as Elvis Presley and his blue suede shoes?"

A week before the Beatles' show, the San Francisco *Examiner* took a poll at a teenage fair at (where else?) the Cow Palace. On the day of the show, they ran the results in an article entitled "Beatles Lose Out To Grubby Stones." The poll found that the Beatles were "slipping in popularity" to the archrival Rolling Stones (the Supremes and Sonny and Cher polled third and fourth, respectively). Other results found teens in favor of mini-skirts, tied on long hair, and against then-candidate for governor, Ronald Reagan (who had stumped through the Bay Area a few days before, saying "one issue overrides the others—the issue of simple morality. We are told that God is dead. Well, He isn't. We just can't talk to Him in our schools.")

At least some things never change.

COW PALACE MEMORIES

Photos from the 1965 shows at the Cow Palace, where Beatlemania reached an all-time fever pitch. The Chronicle *reported, "Most of the teenage girls who broke through the police lines appeared overcome with the nearness to the Beatles and simply swooned to the floor."*

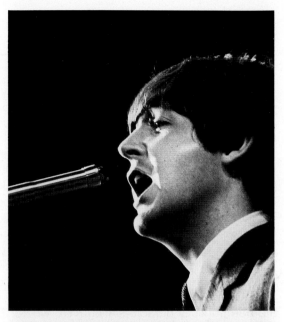

KEEPING TEMPO

In all likelihood, the Beatles were unruffled by the negative press they had generated. Tempo Productions, on the other hand, was not—the local promoters of the upcoming Candlestick Park show were facing the unlikely prospect of *losing* money on a Beatles' concert.

Bobby Mitchell, who co-owned Tempo with Tom Donahue, complained to *Chronicle* columnist Herb Caen: "The most—the MOST—we can make from this gig is $16,000, IF it's a sellout. We have 22,000 tickets sold and we can seat about 30,000. So we could gross $180,000, but let's be more realistic and say $130,000. Those mothers (he means the Beatles—Ed.) take $84,500. The city gets $19,500. Expenses run $20,000 . . . and to top it off the city demands and gets 50 free tickets . . . Geez, I wish I'd never heard of the guys."

For the maverick duo of Donahue and Mitchell, the Beatles' concert was looking more and more like one of their rare financial boondoggles. Since the early Sixties, Tempo had virtually ruled the Bay Area concert circuit, thanks in large measure to the free publicity of radio station KYA, where "Big Daddy" Donahue and "Mighty Mitch" Mitchell moonlighted as popular disc jockeys. The pair's all-star rock'n'soul revues at the Cow Palace— featuring the glittering likes of Marvin Gaye, Martha and the Vandellas, and Little Stevie Wonder (often being backed by a Phil Spector-conducted orchestra)—had been both critical and financial hits.

Donahue and Mitchell had parlayed their concert-promoting profits into an independent record label, Autumn Records, which quickly scored big-time with the Beau Brummels—the first American band to successfully adopt the British Invasion sound (their name, in a wonderfully calculated move, came right after the Beatles in the record stacks). Part of the credit for the Brummels' success—they had two top twenty hits in 1965, "Laugh Laugh" and "Just A Little"—was Autumn Records' house producer, a young disc jockey named Sylvester Stewart (a.k.a. Sly Stone).

The Beau Brummels' stunning success had established Donahue and Mitchell as kingpins of a previously non-existent San Francisco rock community. Under Sly's watchful eye, Autumn soon began to record other homegrown talent, including the proto-psychedelic Great Society (featuring Grace Slick), the Vejtables and even produced a demo for the Emergency Crew (a.k.a. the Grateful Dead). On the

Bob Mitchell (below) presenting Chubby Checker with a plaque at one of Tempo's many successful Cow Palace revues in the early '60s. (Right) Tom "Big Daddy" Donahue, the progenitor of underground FM radio.

concert promotion side, Tempo hosted the Rolling Stones' first concert at the San Francisco Civic Center and later the group's return engagement at the Cow Palace in 1966.

The biggest fish of all, however, had managed to elude Donahue and Mitchell's net: the Fab Four. Initially, Tempo had received verbal agreement to promote the group's pair of 1965 Cow Palace shows, but somehow the contract was handed over to a San Jose promoter named Paul Cattallano. Tempo immediately took legal action against the Beatles for breach of contract, serving them a summons at the Hollywood Bowl one day before the Cow Palace shows.

Raechel Donahue, later "Big Daddy's" wife, recalled the chaotic scene to *BAM* magazine: "The day of the Hollywood Bowl show, we went down to L.A. to serve them with a summons. I was holding this big gold backstage pass and Tom—who was a pretty huge, imposing guy—led the way. No one was going to tell him he couldn't go where he wanted to go. So there we were backstage, and all of a sudden all four Beatles appeared and ran right past us. We couldn't move, didn't say anything. Then they were gone. We finally had to hire a process server."

Eventually, an agreement was worked out between both the Beatles and Tempo's lawyers, whereby Tempo would promote the group's return engagement in 1966. Needless to say, after all the legal expenses to land the Beatles, the entrepreneurial duo of Donahue and Mitchell were far from pleased with the advance gate for the Candlestick show. Despite saving costs by having KYA listeners mail in for their tickets, Tempo was lucky to break even; although one source, whose name has been withheld upon request, claims that Donahue and Mitchell cut their losses by skimming profits from their Sacramento, California ticket outlet. (It is impossible to corroborate the story, however, since both Donahue and Mitchell are dead.)

Still, with whole sections of unsold seats (the eventual total attendance of 25,000 was less than the Beatles' two 1965 shows at the Cow Palace, which drew a combined total of 28,500), it must have been more than a little frustrating for Donahue and Mitchell to witness the parade of bad press in the San Francisco papers. Only one local writer had risen in the group's defense, the *Chronicle's* influential music critic, Ralph J. Gleason. In his column, which appeared on the day of the show, Gleason took dead aim at all the doubters and supposed-soothsayers who had been forecasting the Beatles' imminent decline and fall. The article was called "It's Beatle Day At Candlestick."

John Lennon and Ralph Gleason (right) share a contemplative smoke. One year later, Gleason co-founded Rolling Stone *magazine. The magazine's first cover featured—you guessed it—John Lennon.*

On the Town ||||||||||||||||||||||||||||||||||||||||||||||||||||||||

It's Beatle Day
At Candlestick

|||||||||||||||||||||||||||||||||||||||| **Ralph J. Gleason**

IF YOU SEE a small group of people apparently floating on a raft in the Bay off Candlestick Point late this afternoon, it's John Lennon leading The Beatles across the water from Oakland. They'll be walking, of course. Who has a better right?

Either that or they will arrive in a yellow submarine, boring their way up behind second base.

This is all by way of saying that today is Beatle Day, the day that 50 city officials and/or their friends will have free tickets to the Beatles concert, not as a gift of the promoters, but as part of the rent for the ballpark. Isn't that payola?

Today is also the day that, in addition to $17,500 or 15 per cent of the paid admissions, whichever is greater, the city is collecting $210 for electricity, $35 for water, $25 for gas, $80 for garbage, $270 for washrooms, $145 for toilet paper, $35 for seat covers, $23 for Modess, $21 for borax and $15 for deodorant.

★ ★ ★

ALL THAT, OF COURSE, in addition to $3800 insurance, fees for 200 rent-a-cops, $1260 for special electric power and goodness knows what else.

There will be no press conference here. The Beatles cancelled all but the conferences in Chicago, Nw York, and Los Angeles after their foray into theology and its attendant dispute.

If tonight's concert sells out, there will be 31,000 people there. However, there are still tickets available in the $5 and $6 categories and they will be on sale starting at 10 this morning at Candlestick Park. They will also be on sale until 6 o'clock at KYA. The gates will open for the show tonight at 6:30 and there are special instructions from Police Chief Thomas Cahill for parents or others who schlep their kids over to the park for the show and come back to get them.

Approach Candlestick Park via Ingerson avenue, turning left at Giants' drive, discharging passengers on Giants' drive near the parking lot entrance. Leave via Gilman avenue.

After you get out of Pop's car, you walk through the parking lot to the stadium entrance.

On the return trip, use the same directions.

The Beatles will be the last act in a show which will begin at 8 p.m. with The Remains, a Boston rock group which plays four numbers. Singer Bobby Hebb follows, doing four numbers, including his hit, "Sunny." The Cyrkle is next. This is a new group which had the hit, "Red Rubber Ball," and is managed by Brian Epstein of The Beatles. They do five numbers, including their hit, and are followed by The Ronettes, who sing six numbers, including their big hit, "Da Doo Ron Ron." The show will end by 11 o'clock.

★ ★ ★

THERE WILL BE NO INTERMISSION. Immediately following The Ronrettes, The Beatles will come on stage and the heavens will open and the sky part and the earth tremble.

This is the final concert on this year's Beatle tour, in which they have played 19 shows in 14 cities to fantastic box office grosses (over $250,000 in Los Angeles last night and $300,000 in New York). The Beatles have played to more people this year than ever before, and have played in baseball parks and race courses, as well as arenas, something no entertainment attraction has ever done before.

A curious Yankee backlash has been operating this year against The Beatles. It is almost as if the press and the Adult Numbers want them to fail. Variety reported last week that Herb Alpert had a Toronto sellout, but not The Beatles. Literally true, of course, but Alpert drew 12,800 people in four performances for a $51,427 gross. The Beatles drew 33,500 in two performances for $156,000 gross.

★ ★ ★

It is very hard to admit that the biggest thing in show business is not the circus, Judy Garland, Frank Sinatra (he didn't even sell out the Cow Palace, I seem to remember) or the U.S. Marine Band, but four strange-looking young men from Liverpool who are the greatest song writers since Stephen Foster.

★ ★ ★

JOHN LENNON'S REMARKS about Jesus, for which, as Art Hoppe said, he was promptly crucified, actually served to stimulate the concert box office and increase record sales. The new album, "Révolver," which is the best pop music album I have ever heard and is a remarkable performance, was released the second week of August and has already been certified as selling over $1,000,000 by the Record Industry Association of America. It was tenth best selling album in the country in its second week and is now Number One.

It is just simply a fact of life that nothing has ever been like them. They will take out over $1,000,000 as their end of the 14-city concert tour.

The fuss about Lennon's remark was a symptom of a sick society, really. No radio station which was ever a factor in the pop music field banned The Beatles discs. Only stations which didn't matter banned them. And as for burning the discs, last week it was crosses, this week Beatles records.

So far, Lennon's remarks have been attacked by everybody but the Church, and his critics are in the interesting position of being more righteous than the religious leaders.

★ ★ ★

HIS ANTI-WAR REMARKS (in which his partners joined) haven't been quite as sensational, though no less true and no less important sociologically. It seems to me remarkable that The Beatles see the press at all and are even willing to appear in this country. From Europe's point of view we are wildly violent: mad snipers, rapists, riots, demonstrations, Marines busting picket lines, cops and citizens brawling and the Dallas nightmare of assassination and counter-assassination in the background.

"We would elaborate in England but not here," Paul McCartney said in New York in voicing his anti-war sentiments. "In England, people will listen a bit more to what you say. Here, everything you say is picked up and turned against you."

One final note. Everyone is latching onto the Beatle gravy train. Tonight Del Courtney and 25 musicians will sit in the stands and play the "Star Spangled Banner" for $1072. The promoters were forced to hire them as standby musicians by Local 6 of the American Federation of Musicians, regardless of the AFM members on the show. This is the only city in which this occurred and this is the first time it has happened here in ten years. Originally, the promoters were told specifically who to hire and NOT to hire rock 'n roll musicians. Wow!

INTERVIEW: RAECHEL DONAHUE

Raechel Donahue (above) on the field at Candlestick Park. In 1965, both she and her husband Tom had tried unsuccessfully to serve a summons on the Beatles at their Hollywood Bowl shows.

Raechel Donahue, wife of the late Tom Donahue, helped her husband promote the Beatles' Candlestick Park show. She was later instrumental in establishing the nation's first underground FM station, KMPX in San Francisco. Donahue has also worked as a disc jockey and is currently the host of "On The Flipside," a Los Angeles-based television show.

Q: What were the reasons that the Candlestick Park show was such a financial bust for Tempo?

A: There are a couple different reasons, but the largest one being that the Beatles took sixty-five per cent of the profits.

Q: Didn't KYA help cut the losses by virtue of free promotion?

A: To some degree, yes. We had a special oversized ticket made, which as it turns out did not fit in the ticket counting machines at Candlestick Park. It had lovely pictures of the Beatles, but it doesn't fit in their automatic counter. So all the tickets had to be counted by hand. We did save money by mailing out the tickets from KYA—Tom and his friends and my friends sat in the backroom of KYA licking little envelopes and sending tickets back to people. That was probably the only way we came out even at all, because there was an immense amount of expenses, including 200 rent-a-cops.

Q: I understand you had a problem with the Giant's groundskeeper.

A: Oh yeah, he was hysterical—the man was in tears. Understand that this was before the World Series and he was afraid that there would be bad bounces on the field. In fact, he locked the gates to the grounds because the Beatles were going to go off in an armored car.

Q: Did you have a chance to meet the group?

A: They were not on the grounds very long and we were all pretty busy. Tom's kids got to meet the Beatles, which to the end he maintained was why he did it—it certainly wasn't for the money.

GREETINGS AND SALUTATIONS

Backstage the Beatles obligingly posed for photos and chatted with invited guests. (Right) Joan Baez and Mimi Fariña wait to greet George Harrison.

INTERVIEW: JOAN BAEZ

An internationally-renowned human rights activist, Joan Baez has recorded over thirty albums of folk music. A longtime friend of the Beatles, she was backstage at their final concert. In 1987, Ms. Baez released her autobiography, "And A Voice To Sing With."

Q: When did you first meet the Beatles?

A: They were in Red Rocks, I think it must have been in 1964. Anyway, I sang at Red Rocks one night and they were there the next night, so I stayed over to meet them. There were just thousands of people underneath the catacombs of the Red Rocks trying to meet them. They'd do anything just to feel them. So they came trotting out and said, "Miss Baez, the Beatles want to meet you" and I thought I could have died. I never have had stage fright about meeting anybody.

Q: Are you saying this time you did?

A: Oh, it was ghastly. I was shaking and doing all the appropriate things, thinking this couldn't be me, you know. It's kind of amusing because they seemed a little nervous themselves. I mean they each introduced themselves—"hello, I'm John, hello, I'm Ringo." Here they were on the cover of every newspaper in the country and everybody knew who they were, but I think they were a little nervous, too.

Q: Did you sense a change in the Beatles' attitudes between the different tours?

A: When I first went up to their rooms after the show at Red Rocks, they were very impressionable, very new and excited. They had the radio up because their songs were number one, two, three, four, five, six and seven! And they were knocked out by it all. The one consistent thing is that they were all terribly funny, always, all of them. Wisecracking, wisecracking, wisecracking—really funny.

When I was on tour with them I remember that they were tired. They were more cynical than ever. I remember them saying, "Your bloody American fans are trying to kill us."

Q: I understand you became a security guard for a while?

A: I just assigned myself. I went carting bodies around with this one cop, ushering them over to the Red Cross van. I remember John saying [with a mock Liverpool

On the Beatles legacy, Baez says: "It's a mystical thing to do with the Sixties. They were a first and an original. They were the biggest thing since Elvis and they're the biggest thing since then."

Joan Baez (right) on the Beatles: "The one consistent thing is that they were all terribly funny, always, all of them. Wisecracking, wisecracking, wisecracking—really funny."

accent]: "Oh, there's Miss Florence Nightingale off to the side there."

Q: What do you remember of the Candlestick show?

A: My problem is I don't remember things anymore, it's just this great clutter. I do remember one thing—apparently there was a slight lull in the screaming for about a quarter of a second and Brian Epstein said, "I guess this is our last tour." Because you could almost hear what the Beatles were playing.

Q: Do you think by ending touring that the Beatles began their eventual break-up?

A: I think they were beginning to grow up, which also means break up for a lot of people. I can't imagine trying to last with three people in your life, which is what the public wants. When I say grow up, they went on to different kinds of musical creativity. They had to get out of that scene— that was the bobbysoxer scene. That was just emphasis on screaming and yelling and stardom and crashing limousines. They were more talented than that. They had more work to do.

INTERVIEW: MORT FELD

Mort Feld had the unenviable task of mixing the sound for the Beatles' Candlestick Park show. In 1966, he worked for McCune Audio-Visual, where he is currently vice president. Feld also worked the sound for the 1967 Monterey Pop Festival.

Q: What difficulties did you face setting up the sound for this show?

A: Of course, we were impressed with the importance of the moment even though we didn't know at the time that it was going to be the last concert. After all, these were the world-renowned Beatles. We also knew that we were not going to have a rehearsal or a sound-check—we totally had to wing it. We had a minimum of information and support. They didn't travel with sound people. We also knew that they were going to take into consideration that no one was going to hear, anyhow. That's the way they played it in those days. They just didn't imagine that any sound could work under those conditions, so they didn't care too much about it.   We took everything we owned in the way of loudspeaker equipment. The stage was situated at second base. We put a pile of speakers to the right and a pile of speakers to the left. We also put a cyclone fence around the speakers. There were rumors that the kids might rush the stage and we wanted to protect the equipment, but more importantly, we wanted to protect the kids form getting too close to that terrible amount of sound—which by today's measures was nothing.

Q: What was the onstage sound set up?

A: We put five mikes onstage, no mikes for the instruments. They played through their own amplifiers. The amps scared us because they looked larger than the sound system. We put up mikes for each of them—three mikes across the front—and a big boom mike for Ringo. I remember we had this big studio boom with a counterweight on one end. Ringo came out and on the first number he sat down and playfully swung the boom out and the counterweight came around—so for the balance of the show he sang into the counterweight. So, in effect, we were hardly amplifying Ringo in the mix.

Setting up the sound system during the afternoon of August 29. During the show, Mort Feld, the sound mixer, watched in disbelief as Ringo Starr swung his microphone around and sang into the counterweight.

Otherwise, the sound was relatively good. The mix was not glorious, we had no control over the instruments, just what we could pick up from the vocal mikes, but they could be heard, which no one expected them to be and I was delighted by that. I was mixing from the home dugout.

Q: How about the bootleg tape of the show? Was any tape made off the boards?

A: No, we were too honest and still are. It's just part of our code—we don't make tapes, unless the artist asks us to. I still don't own a tape of that show—and I did the sound mix!

INTERVIEW: MIMI FARIÑA

Mimi Fariña is the founder of Bread and Roses, a non-profit California-based agency that puts together shows for nursing homes, hospitals and prisons. She is also a musician and has recorded several albums, including three with her late husband, Richard Fariña. Like her sister, Joan Baez, Fariña was backstage at the Beatles' last show.

Q: Was this the first time you had seen the Beatles?

A: The first and only.

Q: Your sister Joan Baez mentioned how nervous she was when she first met the Beatles? Did you have a similar reaction?

A: Yes, of course it was exciting, but living with Joan as a sister, many exciting things happened that seemed slightly detached from reality. It was one of many major events that happened in the Sixties. It fit into the scheme of things back then. We didn't sit around and get to gab or become close. I didn't get a chance really to know them. It was sort of like watching a collage, and standing on the sidelines and giggling with my sister and friends and saying: 'Isn't this something?' But there was no real involvement. I think for Joanie there was sincere involvement, talking, getting acquainted, so it had more of an impact, I think, probably, on her.

Q: Coming out of that folk tradition, how did you feel about the Beatles at that time? Did you take it seriously?

A: I think that Richard (Fariña) and I had been growing into a folk rock tendency. After having been to Newport festival, and watching the Butterfield band, and a few other rather radical moves in the folk scene, it was not so new. Plus, the Beatles' playing was not so loud at that time. You could still hear the words, the chords were beautiful, the words said things that we wanted to relate to. So it didn't seem

so far from where we were growing—I'm talking about Richard and me.

Q: And the show itself, do you remember anything about your expectations of a Beatles' show?

A: You're not going to like me for this, but I remember the opening act better, because he sang "Sunny."

Q: Bobby Hebb.

A: Yeah. I just remember hearing that song and being taken by it. I think everything else was so expected. I mean, I was expecting to be rah-rah hearing each Beatles song, and watching the crowd and the teenagers scream and yell, and the flag-waving, and the things they had hanging over the side—"Lennon Saves"—things like that. All that phenomenon was more interesting than the performance, because the event was such a phenomenon.

Q: It sounds sort of anticlimactic.

A: In a way, I mean it was exciting, but I was spoiled. I had been to Joan Baez/Bob Dylan across the country and watched when they sang "Haddie Carroll" in the South and were told not to because they'd be beat up by the Ku Klux Klan—so I had been in pretty intense situations prior to that time that I was much more closely involved with, or related to. This was in a sense a happier event, and bigger in scale, but emotionally, not so new to me. But it was not anticlimactic by any means.

Mimi Fariña (left, in plaid) later told the Chronicle: *"I remember being escorted onto the field and the place sounding like clouds bursting... it was fun. Things were popping. There was a real sense of community then that got dispersed over the years."*

THE LIFE OF BRIAN

As the Beatles and their traveling entourage filed out of their chartered jet in San Francisco, Brian Epstein was back in Los Angeles, the victim of blackmail. One of Epstein's sexual partners had stolen his attaché case (reportedly containing pills and skimmed profits in cash) after a recent tryst in L.A. Already despondent over the group's decision to stop touring, Epstein was now plunged face-first into a deep depression; he would skip the flight to San Francisco. It was a bittersweet irony—the man who had tailored the Beatles' meteoric rise to fame would miss the last chance to see his boys perform.

With or without Epstein, something was bound to go wrong on the Beatles' brief visit to San Francisco (after all, this *was* the tour of '66)—and go wrong it did, as the Beatles found themselves locked out at the front gate of Candlestick Park. Photographer Jim Marshall, who witnessed the absurd turn of events, later recalled: "It was literally a scene out of 'A Hard Day's Night.' We drove around Hunters Point [a neighborhood near Candlestick Park] while teenage girls made kamikaze runs at the bus."

After several minutes of winding around Candlestick Park, the Beatles' entourage was finally let onto the grounds of the baseball park. Immediately, they were confronted by another obstacle, the San Francisco Giants' groundskeeper, who was far from thrilled by the prospect of an armored truck driving over his finely-manicured turf. Eventually, a settlement was worked out, as the vehicle gingerly drove over the foul grounds to the dugout area.

The Beatles took sanctuary in the visiting team clubhouse where they dined on a meal of prime rib of roast beef, Yorkshire pudding, stuffed baked potato, salad, and French pastry. It certainly was an improvement over their regular tour diet. Kenny Everett, a Radio London disc jockey who was reporting on the tour for *Melody Maker* magazine, wrote back, "I can recommend a Beatle tour for one thing—losing weight...we had a steak in Chicago twenty or thirty years ago and since then have been living on cocktail sausage, Coke and Seven-Up."

After the meal was polished off, the band chatted with local newspaper reporters, including Ralph Gleason, and also hobnobbed with an assortment of backstage

In absence of Epstein, Lennon became the group's unofficial mouthpiece. (Left) Beatle John meets the press at Candlestick Park. Asked if the Beatles were borrowing harmonic ideas from the Baroque era, he replied: "I don't know what a baroque is. I wouldn't know a Handel from a Gretel."

guests, including Joan Baez and her sister Mimi Fariña. The group also passed the time by doodling on the tablecloth provided by Simpson's Catering of San Francisco. According to Joe Vilardi, the representative of Simpson's, Lennon sketched a "Japanese sunset in yellow crayon," while McCartney drew "faces in the abstract." (After the show, Vilardi displayed the autographed tablecloth in the window of Simpson's offices. A few days later, the window was shattered in broad daylight by a thief who ran off with the invaluable artifact).

Meanwhile, onstage, the opening acts faced the unenviable task of warming up the chilly Candlestick crowd (the weather forecast for the evening called for variable cloudiness with lows between 50-58, and winds from the northwest at 10 to 20 miles per hour). First up were the Boston - based Remains, who also backed up singer Bobby "Sunny" Hebb. Next were the Cyrkle, Brian Epstein's latest prodigies, with their hit "Red Rubber Ball." Finally, the Ronettes (minus Ronnie Spector, who withdrew from the tour for undisclosed reasons) finished the pre-Beatles festivities. The time was almost at hand.

Backstage, Lennon (right) wore a button that said "Moses." He went around telling everybody, "I've been demoted." (Left) Joan Baez stares at George's doodle.

INTERVIEW: GENE NELSON

Gene Nelson is the morning disc jockey on San Francisco's KSFO/KYA-FM, where he has worked since the mid-Sixties. He, along with Johnny Holiday, was the emcee of the Beatles' Candlestick Park show.

Q: First of all, how did you get the job of emceeing the Beatles' last show?

A: I was working for KYA-AM at the time and we promoted the show. It was a thrill, of course, to be able to emcee the Beatles, although we didn't know quite the import of the show at the time. Nobody knew it was going to be their last one.

Q: Were there any problems emceeing a show of that magnitude?

A: Probably the most difficult thing was that it was outdoors at a ballpark. It's real hard to get any rapport with an audience when you're talking on a microphone at second base. That was a drawback.

Q: Did Candlestick's famous winds create any problems?

A: The wind was so strong that night that it blew the sound towards the East Bay. Of course, nobody came to hear them anyway—they really came just to see them.

Q: Did they seem tired that night?

A: They didn't put much into that show—it only ran about thirty-five minutes. It was short and sweet. I think they were tired and just wanted to get it over with. So as far as shows are concerned, it really wasn't much of a performance. It was more of a happening than a show.

Q: Did you have much contact with the group?

A: They were sealed up in the dressing room while I was out there working with the warm-up acts. So my only contact with them was coming on and off the stage. There was really very little contact with anybody. The thing about the Beatles, they were so big at the time, that even people who were usually blase about performers and shows—like newspaper reporters—were clamoring to get into the dressing room or get a press pass. They had that kind of celebrity status.

(Above) Gene Nelson, the show's emcee, is still a disc jockey at KYA. Brian Epstein's latest prodigies, the Cyrkle (above right), were riding high with their hit, "Red Rubber Ball." (Below right) The Ronettes, minus Ronnie Spector, sing "Be My Baby."

INTERVIEW: VERN MILLER

Vern Miller was the bass player of the Boston-based group, the Remains, who warmed-up for the Beatles 1966 tour. He currently teaches music in a New Jersey junior high school and owns a small recording studio.

Q: Was it much of a problem being the first act at a Beatles show? It almost sounds like a nightmare.

A: Not as much of a problem as we thought it was going to be. In just about all cases we got a really good response. We didn't get the expected "We want the Beatles" cheer, you know. Some of the places even asked for encores. It could have potentially been a very awkward situation, I guess, a very uncomfortable situation to be in, but it actually turned out well. We had a good time playing, and the audiences were very, very receptive.

Q: Did you guys have any chance to intermingle with the Beatles?

A: We travelled together on a chartered plane. I think it was American Airlines, because there was an airline strike at the time. Their management had chartered a jet that the entire tour travelled on all the time, from city to city. Not all the time, but quite a few nights, we stayed in the same hotels. So we would spend some time together then also. One of the big thrills for me was listening to Indian music. Ravi Shankar had given George Harrison some cassettes of sitar lessons, and one of the things that I happened to enjoy the most was going up to George's room a few times and listening to lessons that Shankar had given him to study and listen to while he was on the road.

Q: Did the Beatles' voice their frustrations about touring?

A: It wasn't verbalized. At least, I didn't hear it verbalized. I definitely heard passing comments and the problems about the comment that John had made, involving "We're more popular than Jesus," especially down near the Bible Belt region. I guess there was the possibility of cancelling the Memphis show but it never materialized.

One thing was evident—there was a sense of change in the air. It seemed that Brian Epstein was always very sure to present the Beatles to the public as a unified thing. But it was very evident from being around them that they were very individual,

How do Miller's music students feel about their teacher touring with the Beatles? "When I talk to my kids about it," Miller says "it means so much to me, and it means so much to them. Especially with all this stuff coming out on compact disc—all the teenagers I teach are getting excited about the Beatles again."

The Remains, a Boston-based rock quartet, opened the Beatles' 1966 North American tour dates. Despite the exposure, however, the group (right) broke up shortly after the Beatles tour. (Left to right) Vern Miller, Barry Tashian, Chip Damiani and Bill Briggs.

and that they were perhaps going in different directions. It seems that it was always an effort to get them to appear at the airplane door at the same time together so that they could wave, you know, coming down the stairs of the airplane...not that I think that they didn't like what they were doing—I just got a sense of them being a little bit tired of being Beatles as a group, and perhaps having the desire to be recognized for being themselves.

ONTO THE FIELD

THE LAST SHOW

At 9:27 p.m., the Beatles emerged from the dugout steps of Candlestick Park, guitars and drum sticks in hand, for the short 60-yard stroll over to second base. There waiting for them was an elevated stage—actually a cage—with two fences, a six-foot police barrier and a ten-foot cyclone fence. As usual, the flashbulbs popped and the screamers screamed and rolls of tissue paper flew out of the upper deck. Only the Beatles, themselves, knew that this would be it—their final show after nine years of performing over 1400 concerts.

Dressed in dark green double-breasted Edwardian suits, the group hopped onstage, plugged in, and immediately launched into Chuck Berry's "Rock And Roll Music." In front of the concert speakers was the Beatles' press agent Tony Barrow, who, at the behest of Paul McCartney, was taping the entire performance for posterity. (It is quite likely, in fact, that the widely-circulated bootleg of the Candlestick Park show is the recording that Barrow made).

After a truncated "Rock and Roll Music," the group segued into a gritty, charged-up version of "She's A Woman," proving—once and for all—that when they wanted to, the Beatles could still rock it out like they had in Hamburg and Liverpool. Finishing his bravura turn on vocals, McCartney greeted the crowd and introduced George Harrison to sing "If I Needed Someone"—the only Harrison original to ever be performed on a Beatles' tour.

After Harrison's vocal, Lennon took the microphone, saying, "We'd like to carry on now, carry on together, and will, one together and all for one, with another number that used to be single record...a long time ago. And this one's about the naughty lady called "Day Tripper." Unlike Cleveland, there was no crowd rushing at Candlestick during "Day Tripper"—that was saved for the next selection, "Baby's In Black." *Chronicle* reporter, William Chapin, captured the events in his front page article, "Bedlam at the Ball Park": "At 9:40 p.m., a group of about five boys climbed over a fence from the nearly empty centerfield bleachers and sprinted toward the rear of the infield stage. A covey of private police quickly intercepted them."

Meanwhile, the Beatles, well-protected by 200 guards (some of them ex-Oakland Raider football players), played on distractedly through "Baby's In Black." After the craziness at Dodger Stadium the night before, the band was wary of any

Candlestick Park was characteristically cold on the night of the concert, with lows between 50 and 58 degrees. As for the winds, you don't need a weatherman to know which way the wind blows at Candlestick—it blows in every direction.

The Beatles onstage for the last time together. Lennon later remarked: "What else could we do? Make more money? Play bigger concerts? Go on longer tours?"

potential mayhem—an armored car, with its engine running, was waiting only feet from the stage, just in case things got hairy.

In actuality, the crowd of 25,000 at Candlestick Park had cheered just as loudly for the escaping boys as they had the Beatles. Unlike the incessant roar of past years, the screams for the Beatles were now reserved for the beginning and end of each song. "The fact that the crowd was relatively subdued—in action if not in noise," Chapin theorized in the *Chronicle*, "was at least part attributable to the almost unbelievable set of security measures invoked to keep idols and idolators apart."

The group tried to make up for the enthusiasm-dampening set of circumstances by livening up their microphone chatter with wisecracks and cynical asides. Without Brian Epstein's ever-watchful eye for slips in decorum, the group went a little farther than usual in their stage announcements. Harrison, for example, dryly told the crowd after "Baby's In Black": "We'd like to carry on with something that's very old, indeed. It was recorded in 1959 and it's called 'I Feel Fine'." (It was actually recorded, of course, in 1964.)

Next, McCartney gamely tackled "Yesterday"—a song not exactly suited for windswept outdoor baseball stadiums. After his somewhat strained performance, McCartney acknowledged, "it's a bit chilly," before dedicating the next song, "I Wanna Be Your Man" to "all the wonderful backroom boys on tour."

Ringo Starr could not begin his vocals, however, until he swung the microphone stand around (his drumming, thus far, had been inaudible to the Candlestick crowd). Starr's frustration may have had something to do with the fact that the Beatles had never worked up a live presentation of his then-hit vocal on "Yellow Submarine." Earlier in the tour, he had explained to some fans backstage why the "Eleanor Rigby"/"Yellow Submarine" single was not being performed on tour: "To be honest, we've kept the same list of titles we used last month in Germany and the Far East. We haven't had the chance to rehearse any new numbers since then."

The screams Starr generated with his umpteenth—although still crowd-pleasing—version of "I Wanna Be Your Man" quickly died down as Harrison, McCartney and Lennon intoned the three-part a cappella intro to "Nowhere Man." But the wistful mood of the song was shattered by another "raiding party" of teenage boys, who had jumped over the outfield fence with security in close pursuit. This time,

A bird's eye view of the Beatles onstage at Candlestick Park. The distance between the Beatles and their fans had never been greater. The closest spectator was over two hundred feet away.

the Beatles were audibly annoyed by the gate crashers; McCartney got on the microphone after the song had finished, saying, "We'd like to carry on, I think—nobody's sure yet . . . well, should we just watch this for a minute?"

As though to reprimand the audience (who cheered wildly for the escaping boys), the band launched into a ragged, out-of-tune version of "Paperback Writer." Afterwards, with only one song to go, the band took more liberties at the mike stand. Lennon told the audience, "thank you very much everybody—everybody's wonderful in Frisco" to which Harrison added "bitchin'." Finally, trying to salvage the situation, McCartney announced, "We'd like to say it's been wonderful being here in this wonderful sea air. Sorry about the weather. We'd like to ask you to join in and clap, sing, talk, do anything...good night."

The band then kicked out one last version of Little Richard's "Long Tall Sally"—a surprise replacement for "I'm Down," the tour's usual set-closer. As the Beatles finished the song, yet another boy jumped onto the ballpark field, momentarily drawing the audience's attention away from an historical moment—the Beatles' final song in concert. As the crowd cheered the escaping boy on, the Beatles quickly filed offstage and into the awaiting armored car. Just before leaving, one of the Beatles (most likely Lennon) mischievously strummed the opening guitar figure of "In My Life," but it was just a tease—even if they had wanted to, the Beatles could not have played the unrehearsed number.

Before the crowd realized what had happened, the Beatles, ensconced safely in the Loomis truck, had disappeared into a cloud of dust. The truck raced out of Candlestick Park, escorted by eleven San Francisco motorcycle cops, as the audience looked on, stunned by the abruptness of the group's exit. The Beatles' entire visit to San Francisco had lasted five hours.

All together now: Candlestick Park was the last public concert the Beatles gave. Almost three years later the group showed up on the rooftop of Apple, but they could never get back to where they once belonged.

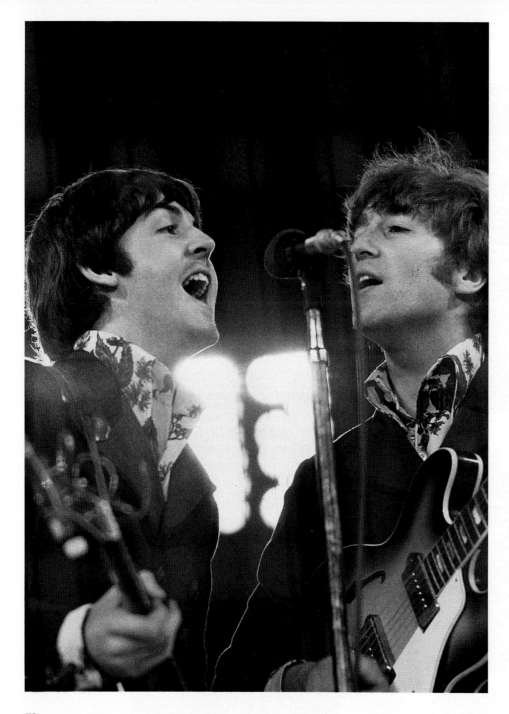

The greatest songwriting team in modern history share a microphone one last time in concert. Earlier in the tour McCartney had remarked, "In America they hold everything you say against you," to which Lennon replied, "You'll have to answer for that tomorrow."

Ringo Starr: "I sometimes do . . . think I'm a bit old to be going onstage doing this. Then I look around at all the other people doing the same and I don't feel so bad."

Philip Elwood (above) was critical of the fact that the Beatles did not perform any material off Revolver: *"I was very annoyed at that because my two daughters who I brought to the show expected those songs and were really disappointed. I think a lot of people were disappointed."*

INTERVIEW: PHILIP ELWOOD

Philip Elwood has been a music critic at the San Francisco Examiner since 1965. He also hosts his own radio show on San Francisco's non-profit KPFA. Elwood reviewed the Candlestick Park show for the Examiner.

Q: Was this your first Beatles' show?

A: I had seen them at the afternoon Cow Palace show in 1965, but I didn't review them because that evening I saw Judy Garland. So I had the Beatles in the afternoon and Judy Garland at night.

Q: Did you discern many differences between the Cow Palace and Candlestick Park shows?

A: They were entirely different situations. Indoors, in the afternoon, is quite a different scene than outdoors at night where the closest person is the equivalent of being in a box seat at a baseball game—that's as close as anybody was. Furthermore, the wind was blowing quite severely—Candlestick Park has a tendency to have hard-blowing winds. Even with binoculars it was hard to see.

It was much more exciting in the afternoon at the Cow Palace—they had a lot more spirit. But that isn't really fair—outdoors in a ballpark they were cold, the wind was blowing, they were two hundred feet away from the closest spectators, so what could you expect?

Q: Do you think it was tactical mistake by the Beatles to play this type of venue?

A: It wasn't a tactical mistake for them, it was just a matter of bad placing. In most cities in August, the evening is balmy, but in San Francisco, it's one of the coldest, foggiest months. I'm sure if anybody had really given a damn, somebody would have told them.

Q: Was it disappointing that they played no songs off *Revolver*?

A: It sure was. I was very annoyed at that because my two daughters who I brought to the show expected those songs, and were really disappointed. And I think a lot of people were disappointed. But, after all, this was the end of their tour. I doubt very much that they changed anything in their show from city to city.

Q: Where do you think this show falls in their history?

A: I have a feeling that the wear and tear of that tour and the obvious personal frictions that were developing, particularly between Lennon and McCartney, were accentuated by being on the road together. I think they all realized that if they kept touring very much longer the whole thing was going to fall apart. Anyway, if seeing the Beatles live on tour meant going out to Candlestick Park, I think it was probably good for everybody that they did stop touring.

Beatles Strike Out at Ball Park

By PHILIP ELWOOD

Precisely 30 minutes and 11 tunes after they mounted their caged performance tower over second base at Candlestick Park last night the Beatles cascaded downward into a revved up armored truck and vanished behind a cloud of right field dust into the night.

Some 25,000 spectators, exhilarated and excited, were left much like a jammed ballpark crowd that had just seen the winning homerun ball disappear into the bleachers: numbed by the sudden end of the spectacle and disappointed by the brevity of the climactic event.

Master of ceremonies Gene Nelson had earlier joked, "with the breezes out here you will see The Beatles but they may hear them better in Alameda." A funny line (one of many by Nelson and Johnny Holiday) but inaccurate: everyone could hear most of the Beatles' songs, if at times drowned by screams, but none of the paying customers could see clearly or feel any personal involvement with the four young Englishmen in the distance.

The concert, as such, must be termed a bust. Sure, Paul McCartney's remarkably pure tenor on "Yesterday" was good to hear; "I Wanna Be Your Man," "Day Tripper," "Paperback Rider" and the others came out just like on the records: but concerts, even by the Beatles, should mean more than four little figures far away creating wind-distorted sounds inferior in quality to the totally familiar studio recorded versions.

Ringo's drums, such as they are, were inaudible, and we didn't even get his hilarious vocal on "Yellow Submarine"... it wasn't included. As a matter of fact nothing from the new delightful album was on the show, probably because special sound effects and backgrounds are impossible in ballpark appearances.

For thousands of expectant youngsters, once the thrill of the Beatles actually running out of the dugout and onto the stand had worn off, the principal diversion came in cheering the beginning of each two minute tune and then watching the boys who broke through the centerfield fence as they played tag with the police. A good portion of the crowd even missed the Beatles split-second disappearing act because they were absorbed in watching four husky guards wrestle a young Amazon to the turf.

It was, of course, a fascinating evening from a spectator's point of view: observing the colorful crowd, not the stage. Perhaps that is what much of Beatlemania, and similar addictions, is all about. Being there is what counts to the kids, not the possibility of acquiring more familiarity with the performers because of closer personal contact.

The whole evening's production was an expensive and thoroughly synchronized bit of highly commercial machinery. Each of the preliminary throw-away acts did their stint to indifferent crowd response, and soaked up the minutes until the Beatles appeared. Then came the screams, the thousands of flash-bulbs (God knows what those little cameras captured from 100 yards away) ... and for a half hour it happened.

Reprinted by permission.   © San Francisco Examiner, 1966.

The Beatles' gentle giant roadie, Mal Evans (left), puts the squeeze on Joan Baez while the Beatles play on stage. In Cincinnati, Evans had been thrown twenty feet from an electrical shock he received from plugging in the Beatles' amps during a rainstorm.

At the end of "Long Tall Sally," another boy escaped onto the field, pursued by a few of the 200 rent-a-cops in true Keystone Cop fashion. The Beatles became annoyed by the antics—they made a quick exit by armored car while the crowd cheered the boy on.

WEDNESDAY, AUGUST 31, 1966

On the Town

A Puppet Show For the Beatles

Ralph J. Gleason

THE BEATLES entered Candlestick Park Monday evening like a scene out of "A Hard Day's Night."

Their caravan of a Loomis armored car, a huge rented bus and several autos, was preceded by a police station wagon and it raced along the peripheral road at the edge of the Candlestick Park parking lot, cool as a freight train. No one would know it was the Beatles.

No one but the several hundred kids in the parking lot at 5:45 who promptly raced towards the gate to meet them. The three-car caravan, with a couple of extra police on tricycles, got into the parking lot and sped towards the right-field gate of the stadium.

★ ★ ★

IT SEEMED as if it were all directed by Richard Lester. The guard couldn't open the padlock on the chain that barred the entrance to the huge pink sliding door to let the truck and the bus and the cars into the stadium. So they circled around a set of dodgem cards at Playland-at-the-Beach, while the kids ran screaming after them and a couple of sprinters jumped on the back of the armored car and hung on precariously.

A big sedan rushed up, brakes squealing. "Follow the bus!" yelled a man to the driver of the armored car and the entourage sped off, out the parking lot to the road that runs around it and went off south of the stadium. More police raced up and someone finally unlocked the chain and the Beatles transport convoy came around again, speeding along the outside road, and ran up to the pink door and slowly got inside, one vehicle at a time. Two Volkswagens which were riding the tail of the armored car were stopped at the last minute from slipping through the gate after the Beatles.

"I saw him, I saw him" a girl sobbed, her bellbottoms flapping in the wind. We never learned whom she meant.

★ ★ ★

TV CAMERAMEN set up an impromptu interview with a mob of teenie-boppers carrying signs and wearing "I Love Paul" buttons.

Inside, the crowd slowly filled the seats, all but a section out past first base. They were orderly enough and greeted the other acts on the show politely, which was generous because the show preceding the Beatles was the dullest to play here in years. The sound system, a cluster of huge speakers set at an angle off the stage worked well and the singers were audible, if distorted, and there was no wind.

Then the Beatles came on and the kids screamed and rolls of tissue went flying onto the field and the girls jumped up and waved and screamed and screamed. Two stalwart groups of youths, raiding parties actually, climbed the centerfield fence and ran on the field in a glorious game of tag with the police. We all rooted for the kids to win, and they did, even though they were caught in the end. The cops merely hustled them into the stands.

★ ★ ★

AND THEN it was over, the shortest rock concert I ever attended. The eleven songs The Beatles sang (all but the opening "Rock 'n' Roll Music" and the closing "Long Tall Sally" were their own compositions) went quickly and by 10 o'clock they were in their armored car speeding off to the airport while the cops carried a girl through the stands on a stretcher and kids ran up and down the aisles waving banners and signs, and puffs of wind blew clouds of dust across the infield.

Is it all worth it? As a spectacle it is not without sociological interest, of course. As a performance it is, like John Lennon says, a puppet show. It can hardly continue to be attractive to four such rational, intelligent and talented human beings.

"NO DOWNFALL FOR US"

Flying back that night of August 29, down the coastline to Los Angeles, the Beatles were not in a celebratory mood. Exhausted from the fiasco of their third and final North American tour, they were lost in private contemplation about the future. From this moment on, life would change immeasurably for each of the Beatles—touring, which had been their full-time occupation for so many years, would forever cease. They were suddenly individuals again.

Of all the Beatles, George Harrison had grown to dislike the rigors of touring the most. On the flight back to Los Angeles, he reportedly announced, "So it's all over. I can stop pretending to be a Beatle now, people!" (this according to Tony Barrow's tour journal later printed in "The Beatles Book" fan magazine).

On the 1966 summer tour, Harrison had whiled away his free moments listening to, and studying, tapes of Ravi Shankar's sitar music. What had started as a dilettante's dabbling in Indian music would soon become a full-blown passion for Harrison. Following the tour, he would fly off to India to study sitar under the personal tutelage of Shankar.

John Lennon took even less time off—approximately four days—before flying off to Germany to begin filming Richard Lester's "How I Won The War." "I was always waiting for a reason to get out of the Beatles from the day I made 'How I Won The War' in 1966," Lennon later told *Newsweek*. "I just didn't have the guts to do it, you see. Because I didn't know where to go. I remember why I made the movie. I did it because the Beatles had stopped touring and I didn't know what to do."

Apparently, acting did not alleviate Lennon's dilemma; he later admitted he was bored silly by the process of filmmaking. The bored Beatle did manage to use some of his idle time on location well, however. Between shoots, he constructed a new song on his acoustic guitar called "Strawberry Fields Forever." Later, back in London, Lennon met an artist named Yoko Ono at her "Unfinished Paintings and Objects" show.

Paul McCartney, it seems, was more bothered by the prospect of ending touring than the others. Certainly, he was the most defensive about the supposed decline in the Beatles' popularity. "There'll be no downfall for us," he told *Melody Maker* after the group returned to London. "We're not worried, we don't dread it. When we get sick of all the hocus pocus and the press and the screaming, we'll just take a fat holiday on our fat wallets." And that is exactly what McCartney did after the tour— he left on an African safari with longtime Beatle comrade Mal Evans.

Despite the rioting in Germany, the ugly airport skirmish in the Philippines, the death threats in Memphis and the risk of electrocution in Cincinnati and St. Louis, McCartney had not grown sick of the worship and adulation that came with Beatlemania. Then again, he remained the sole bachelor within the group—despite rumors to the contrary.

Ringo Starr, on the other hand, had become a father to Zak, his first child with wife Maureen. After the tour had finished, the ever-down-to-earth drummer spent time at home getting to know his son. Even Ringo, it seems, had had enough of touring. With his drumming thoroughly lost in the sound mix of outdoor baseball parks, he had had to be content to smile at the faraway faces and wait for his one turn in the spotlight. Still, perhaps the idea of finishing live performances altogether had not quite sunk in. Backstage at Candlestick Park, Starr had told a New York *Times* reporter that "the group had no plans for retirement and would continue to perform as long as they were in demand."

Starr was not alone. Brian Epstein had also not given up completely on future touring plans, as evidenced in his press statement at the group's recent Dodger Stadium show. Deep down, however, Epstein knew the truth— and it troubled him. "Brian was very sad and almost pathetic," Nat Weiss, lawyer and friend of Epstein, later told Hunter Davies about the manager's post-touring days. "He suddenly said, 'What do I do now? What happens to my life?'" Tragically, on August 27, 1967, almost a year to the day of the Candlestick Park show, Epstein died of overdose of sleeping pills.

TOMORROW NEVER KNOWS

"Whate'er the course, the end is the renown."

—*William Shakespeare*
All's Well That Ends Well

"I'd like to see some more of America . . . it's the kind of place that might blow up some day."

—*John Lennon*
Melody Maker (9-3-66)

Although it was not readily apparent at the time, the Beatles' final show at Candlestick Park had become a pivotal moment in the course of their history and eventual demise. Specifically, in terms of Beatles history, it represented the end of Beatlemania. Touring had bonded the Beatles together since the days of Hamburg, when they were a band of hell-bent Liverpool scruffs. But by 1966, world weariness had worn down the innocence and, gradually, their camaraderie as well.

Even before the 1966 tour, a wistful-tinged nostalgia for the past had cropped up in songs such as "In My Life" and "Yesterday". The "I," "Me," "She" and "You" songs ("I Want To Hold Your Hand," "Love Me Do," "She Loves You") of their earlier years had faded into the cynicism of "Taxman," the sadness of "Eleanor Rigby" and the detached longing on "She Said, She Said."

The mere idea, however, that a group could end all live appearances was somewhat extraordinary—if not unprecedented. Sure, Elvis had taken a break from the stage, but he still cranked out two or three movies a year. The Beatles, however, faced a two-level problem. First of all, the fan adoration had made life on tour intolerable. Secondly, their music had grown leaps and bounds beyond their performance capabilites. Ultimately, the only solution for the group was to retreat to the seclusion of the recording studio.

George Melly, a noted jazz singer and critic, later wrote about this turning point in Beatles history in his book, "Revolt Into Style": "Their [the Beatles] opting out of touring was in itself an affirmation of their determination to prove their self-sufficiency as artists. To paraphrase Cezanne, they hoped to make pop 'solid like the art in museums.'"

When the Beatles finally did go back into the studio in December, 1966— after a (then-record) five month lay-off between recordings—they dug deep into their Liverpool memories, recording the brilliant single, "Penny Lane"/"Strawberry Fields Forever" (along with the later-to-be-released, "When I'm Sixty-Four").

They were songs about lost innocence, pungent yearnings to return to a simpler era. But the Beatles could not return—not to Liverpool, nor to Hamburg, nor to "yeah, yeah, yeahs" and screaming. By 1967, other groups, such as the made-for-TV Monkees, had filled the mania gap (interestingly, "The Monkees" TV show debuted only two weeks after the Beatles' final concert at Candlestick Park). Meanwhile, in San Francisco, and other selected pockets in the universe, the sounds of psychedelia were revolutionizing a new generation of tuned-in and turned-on music listeners.

The Beatles' response was to drop out. After months of laboring and secrecy, they resurfaced in June, 1967, in full regalia as a shadow band named "Sgt. Pepper's Lonely Hearts Club Band." In a shrewd bit of packaging, the Beatles had managed to provide their public with an entire tour (a tack they would later try to duplicate, unsuccessfully, with the film "Magical Mystery Tour"). From the crowd noises at *Sgt. Pepper's* beginning to the crescendo-finale of "A Day In The Life," the listener was capitivated and spellbound as if they were at a live performance. Leaving nothing to chance, the liner notes on the back cover said, "a splendid time is guaranteed for all."

And, yet, the years have not been kind to *Sgt. Pepper*. Somehow it now seems a bit forced, as if studio perfectionism had gotten the best of the group. In "Revolt Into Style," Melly writes "listening again to 'Sergeant Pepper' now that its electrifying novelty has worn off, what strikes me as so interesting is that it is finally a celebration of the past with its certainties and simplicities."

In many ways, the Beatles' history after the Candlestick Park show was, indeed, a frustrating and finally unsuccessful search for the magic that had skyrocketed the group to unheard-of levels of riches and fame; although, technically, the Candlestick Park show is not the last public performance the Beatles ever gave. On June 25, 1967, they sang "All You Need Is Love" via satellite to a worldwide audience; and in 1968 performed "Hey Jude" to a studio audience on the "David Frost Show."

The Loomis armored car kept its engine running throughout the entire Beatles concert—just in case. Earlier in the tour, Time *magazine had commented that "the Beatles' trip to Shea Stadium by armored truck seemed dictated more by showmanship than necessity." They obviously hadn't attended the show in Cleveland.*

Ringo Starr makes a quick getaway to the the armored car. Just before leaving stage, one of the Beatles (most likely John Lennon) strummed the opening chords to "In My Life." It was a private little joke for the 25,000 fans in attendance.

Finally, on January 30, 1969, the Beatles showed up in public for the last time for the infamous rooftop show of the Apple Records building at 3 Savile Row. The idea, of course, was to "Get Back" to the basics, as the foursome attempted to capture the excitement that a only a live performance could inject into a recording. But in reality, the situation was just a sad paradigm of the Beatles' situation—they could not go back, no matter how long and hard they labored, the distance was too great. Playing on a rooftop was really just a private joke.

Ultimately, the actual break-up of the band was precipitated by McCartney's suggestion to Lennon that the group should attempt an impromptu tour of small clubs. Lennon's response—"I think you're daft"—signaled the true end. The divorce papers were filed.

The four Beatles, individually, did not cease live performances, however; each ex-member, it seemed, needed to experience the euphoric rush of the stage one more time. Lennon showed up at the Toronto Rock'n'Roll Festival to growl, "Money" and later, in his last performance, joined Elton John at Madison Square Garden for "Lucy In The Sky With Diamonds" and "I Saw Her Standing There."

George Harrison, who vetoed the group's proposed live TV special to be filmed in Africa, was surprisingly active in his post-Beatles performances, organizing the Bangla Desh benefit concerts and taking on a full-scale, though fairly disastrous, tour of the States in 1974. In 1985, Harrison showed up at the taping of the "Carl Perkins and Friends" TV special, where he sang the old Beatles/Perkin's cover, "Everybody Wants To Be My Baby."

Ringo Starr, as usual, was ready and willing to show up where he was wanted—at the Bangla Desh shows and the Band's "Last Waltz" shows in San Francisco's Winterland Arena. In 1985, Starr joined Harrison on the delightful Carl Perkins' show, singing "Honey Don't."

Not suprisingly, the one who enjoyed touring the most—or should we say hated it the least—has been the most active, and successful, performer in his post-Beatle career: Paul McCartney. Eventually, McCartney carried out his dream of showing up at undisclosed venues with his new group, Wings, who did a mini-tour of British colleges in the early '70s. Later, in 1976, McCartney launched the box-office busting "Wings Over America" tour, which featured performances of several Beatles classics, including "I've Just Seen A Face," "The Long And Winding Road," "Lady Madonna," and "Yesterday."

In more recent years, McCartney has shown up to sing "Let It Be" at the Live Aid concerts in 1985 and, in 1986, joined performers onstage at Prince Philip's charity birthday celebration to sing "Get Back", "I Saw Her Standing There" and "Long Tall Sally" (the concert-closer at Candlestick Park).

As for the public, the rumors are always rife that the three remaining Beatles will show up onstage somewhere, somehow, someday. Certainly, interest in seeing the Beatles live has never ebbed. In fact, one of the most successful post-Beatles record releases was "The Beatles At The Hollywood Bowl" album, released in 1977. Many bootlegs of Beatle performances have also circulated among collectors.

Any chances for a live reunion, of course, were extinguished on December 8, 1980. Without John Lennon there can be no true reunion—after all, who would provide the quotes? Even in the most trying moments on tour, Beatle John could always be counted on for a well-placed barb or quip to break the tension. One week before the group left on their ill-fated 1966 tour, Lennon submitted to one of *Melody Maker's* call-and-response "Pop Think In" interviews. The last few questions went as follows:

THE BOMB

Should be bombed.

WINE

And women.

JAGGER

A good nut.

AMERICA

Great possibilities.

LIFE AND DEATH

Time I was on stage.

Before the crowd realized what had happened the Beatles had disappeared into a cloud of dust. Their last visit to San Francisco had lasted approximately five hours.

JIM MARSHALL started his photography career in 1960. Since then he has photographed over 500 album covers and documented music festivals ranging from Monterey Pop and Woodstock to Altamont. He also covered the Civil Rights movement in 1963/64 and his photos of Appalachia are in the Smithsonian Institute's permanent collection. He lives in San Francisco.

ERIC LEFCOWITZ is a San Francisco-based writer who specializes in "pop archeology." He has published articles in the San Francisco *Chronicle, Boston Rock* and *Caribbean Travel and Life.* This is his second book.